Hansi and the Iceman

Julia Taylor Ebel

Illustrated by Idalia Canter

This is a story about change. What changes could you tell a story about?

Julia Taylor Ebel

Text copyright © 2014 by Julia Taylor Ebel
Illustrations copyright © 2014 by Idalia Canter
All Rights Reserved

Parkway Publishers, Inc.
Blowing Rock, NC

Title Calligraphy by John Stevens
Book design by Aaron Burleson, spokesmedia

Printed in China

Library of Congress Cataloging-in-Publication Data

Ebel, Julia Taylor.
  Hansi and the ice man / by Julia Taylor Ebel ; illustrated by Idalia Canter.
       pages cm
  Includes bibliographical references and index.
  Summary: "As Mr. O'Malley cuts ice blocks for iceboxes, chips fly. Hansi and his friends cluster around Mr. O'Malley's horse-drawn delivery wagon to eat those chips. When Hansi's grandmother trades her icebox for a refrigerator, Hansi worries that Mr. O'Malley will soon stop delivering ice. Includes endnotes and historical photographs"--Provided by publisher.
  ISBN 978-1-933251-81-3 (alk. paper)
  1. Ice industry--United States--History--Juvenile literature. 2. Refrigerators--History--Juvenile literature. 3. Horse-drawn vehicles--United States--Juvenile literature. 4. German Americans--Juvenile fiction. I. Canter, Idalia, ill. II. Title.
  HD9481.U3E24 2013
  333.91'22--dc23
                                                            2013004368

Adapting to a New Culture

Hansi and the Iceman takes place in a period just following a peak in European immigration to America. Throughout history, immigrants have adapted to new lifestyles and language at different rates; but children, especially in American-born generations, often adapt most easily.

While children's names often reflect family members' names, those names can change over time. For example, many young men named *Johannes* or *Hans* became known as *John*, replacing the Germanic version of the name. *Hansi* (pronounced *Hän´-sē*) is a nickname for Johannes or Hans.

Ice harvesting, sawing, c. 1900-1910
Library of Congress, Prints & Photographs Division,
Detroit Publishing Company Collection, LC-D4-30864

Ice harvesting, barring off, c. 1900-1906
Library of Congress, Prints & Photographs Division,
Detroit Publishing Company Collection, LC-D4-17130

In memory of John
and for his family
and for all who remember
the iceman and his chips

—JTE

For my son Matthew,
who asked his grandparents
to tell him stories of the old days

—IC

John Stevens graciously contributed the title lettering as a tribute to John Ebel,
lifetime learner and student of calligraphy.

"I-i-ice-man!" Mr. O'Malley called. His horse-drawn wagon rolled around the corner and down the street.

Clip-clop, clip-clop.

Hansi heard the call, the clatter, and the rhythm of hoofbeats.

"Mattie, whoa," Mr. O'Malley signaled to his horse.

Hansi and Elizabeth dashed down the steps to meet the ice wagon.

The iceman stopped
near Oma and Opa's house,
where Hansi's family lived with
his grandmother and grandfather.

"Hallo-o-o!"
Mr. O'Malley greeted Hansi and Elizabeth with his usual sweeping wave.

"Hello, Mr. O'Malley!" Hansi called.

From up the street, Karl, Anna, and Tony ran to meet Mr. O'Malley's ice wagon.

"Stand back a bit, now." Mr. O'Malley struck a long block of ice again and again with his pick.

Ice chips scattered.

Hansi cupped his hands,
ready to catch an ice sliver.

"Catch one for me," Elizabeth said.

Hansi tried to grab the flying ice chips. At last, he caught one. The ice cooled his hand. "For you." He dropped the chip onto Elizabeth's palm.

She slipped the ice into her mouth.

Mr. O'Malley tapped the ice until he broke away a big block. He gripped the ice block with wide tongs and hoisted it onto a leather pad that covered his shoulder.

While Mr. O'Malley carried ice into Mrs. Stein's house, Hansi and his friends gathered ice chips that had fallen on the wagon bed. Hansi slid chips between his fingers and into his mouth. He let the ice melt against his warm tongue.

As Mr. O'Malley returned to his wagon, Hansi glanced at the sign in Oma's window. "Twenty-five pounds," he said.

Mr. O'Malley cut a block of ice.

"How do you know where to cut?" Hansi asked.

"Practice," Mr. O'Malley said with a wink. He squeezed his big tongs around the ice and hooked the handle onto his hanging scales.

He nodded. "Twenty-five pounds."

Again, Mr. O'Malley swung the ice over his leather-draped shoulder. Then he carried the ice through the back door into Oma's kitchen.

Hansi and Elizabeth followed him.

Mr. O'Malley lifted the ice into the metal ice compartment inside the wooden cabinet.

"*Das reicht. Danke schoen,*" Oma said, handing him her ice coupon in payment.

"That is enough. Thank you," Hansi repeated to Mr. O'Malley.

Mr. O'Malley hurried back to his wagon. He clutched the reins beneath Mattie's chin. "Mattie, get-up," he said softly, walking beside her.

Mattie gently inched the wagon along the street. She stopped and waited at each house as Mr. O'Malley carried ice inside.

One day, Oma made an announcement. "I am getting an electric icebox—a refrigerator. It will keep my food cold without ice. Imagine that!" Oma smiled broadly.

"Ah, that's good!" Momma said.

"No ice?" Hansi asked.

"*Kein Eis*, no ice," Oma said. "No more melting ice drip-dripping like rain into the pan under the icebox. Oh, so messy to empty!"

"No more ice?" Elizabeth asked with a frown.

"No more ice. We'll plug the electrical cord into the wall—like a lamp—and the refrigerator will keep our food cold." Oma nodded firmly.

Hansi wondered if the neighbors would buy refrigerators too. What would happen to Mr. O'Malley and his ice wagon… and Mattie?

And he wondered about ice chips.

Oma's refrigerator came on a shiny truck, not on a horse-drawn wagon. Hansi watched as deliverymen carried the refrigerator inside. He watched them load the old icebox onto the truck bed. They tied the icebox in place with a rope and drove away.

"Where is our icebox going?" Hansi asked.

"To somebody nearby who needs an icebox," Oma said.

Oma placed milk, bratwurst, and cheese in her refrigerator.

Hansi reached inside, too. Already, he could feel cool air.

"Look," Oma said. "We'll make our own ice now." She filled a metal tray with water and slid it into a small metal box inside the refrigerator.

Hansi looked at Oma's refrigerator with its humming motor perched on top—like a head, he thought.

The next day, Hansi heard Mr. O'Malley's ice wagon rattling down the street. He ran out the front door—but stopped.

Hansi looked over his shoulder at Oma's window. The "Ice Today" sign was gone. Instead, Elizabeth watched silently from the window.

Hansi knew that Mr. O'Malley was not coming for Oma now—not for him, not for Elizabeth.

He watched as his friends ran to greet Mr. O'Malley.

If only Oma hadn't bought that refrigerator, he could still catch ice chips with his friends.

Mr. O'Malley looked up at Hansi.
"You'd better come get some chips," he said.

"But Oma won't be buying ice anymore."
Hansi hung his head.

"Come on," Mr. O'Malley said with a welcoming wave of his muscular arm.

Hansi saw Elizabeth's hopeful look. He nodded to her and darted down the steps just as he had always done. Elizabeth raced behind him.

Hansi, Elizabeth, and their friends gathered chips while Mr. O'Malley delivered ice along their street.

As Mr. O'Malley drove on, the friends followed Hansi and Elizabeth inside to see Oma's new refrigerator.

Oma smiled as she opened the refrigerator door and let cold air drift out.

"It makes ice," Hansi said.

Oma showed his friends the tray filled with ice. Anna edged closer, Tony stood on tiptoes, and Karl peered over Anna's shoulders.

Then Oma poured a little raspberry syrup into five glasses and added cool water.

"Raspberry syrup!" Hansi said. He remembered helping Momma and Oma pick their prized red raspberries.

Oma winked at him and then handed each child a raspberry drink—a perfect summer treat.

And Momma even offered warm oatmeal cookies.

"*Danke!*" Hansi said,

"Thank you!" the others echoed.

Hansi looked over his glass at Elizabeth as he sipped his raspberry treat.

"Ice from Mr. O'Malley, still, and raspberry drink with cookies, all in the same day."

Hansi smiled and then said…

"And now Mr. O'Malley takes ice to our old icebox at someone else's house."

Elizabeth grinned.
"All in the same day."

A Need for Ice and Cooling

We open the refrigerator door and place food inside to keep it cool and fresh. Easy. Through the years, people have preserved food in various ways. Salted meats and brine-soaked vegetables can be kept longer than fresh meat or produce. Canning and freezing also preserve food, but freezing requires refrigeration.

Until refrigeration was available, people used natural methods to keep foods cool and fresh. Springs bring a flow of cool underground water to the surface. Warm milk spoils quickly, but a springhouse built over a flowing spring makes a cool place to store a crock of milk. Cellars dug into the ground provide cool storage for produce.

Ice cut from frozen lakes and ponds also has kept food cool. Iceboxes were built as wooden cabinets with metal-lined compartments, one for food and one for ice to cool the food. As the ice melted, it dripped into a pan beneath the icebox.

Icebox: photo by author, used with permission of the Henry Ford Museum

GE Monitor Top refrigerator: photo by author, used with permission of the Henry Ford Museum and General Electric Company

While ice from lakes and ponds was available in colder regions, hauling ice to warmer climates was a challenge. On warm days, ice could melt quickly, even in northern regions. To limit melting, ice was packed in sawdust for delivery to homes.

As populations grew and northern rivers and lakes became polluted, finding a new source of clean ice became necessary. Refrigeration was devised for ice plants that made ice and stored it for delivery to home iceboxes. Later, home refrigerators were marketed.

The refrigerator in the story is a General Electric Monitor Top Refrigerator, a popular early refrigerator, introduced in 1927 and produced with similar design until 1936. While it was said to be the first affordable refrigerator for the home, it cost between $200 and $500—no small price at that time.

Icemen, Ice Chips, and Children

In towns and cities, icemen drove horse-drawn wagons through the neighborhoods. The iceman read a sign left in a window to show how much ice the resident needed. Even after delivery trucks became available, many ice companies found horses better suited to deliveries with frequent stops.

Icemen traveled with several tools:

- An ice pick broke ice into blocks.
- Tongs gripped ice blocks for lifting and carrying.
- Scales verified an iceman's accuracy in cutting ice, in case a customer questioned a weight.
- A leather or rubber ice apron protected the iceman's shoulder and back as he carried ice. Some aprons had pockets to catch drips.

Ice wagon and Horse, Dade City, Florida: Courtesy of East Pasco Historical Society

Ice delivery wagon, Chapel Hill, NC, 1927: North Carolina Collection, University of North Carolina, Library at Chapel Hill

Across the country, the arrival of the ice wagon brought children running to gather ice chips. This story was inspired by memories from my father-in-law. He, Elizabeth, and their siblings, were the first American-born generation from a German immigrant family living in Jackson Heights, New York. In 1927, his grandmother's new refrigerator attracted curious neighbors, friends, and relatives.

Every generation sees change as knowledge, invention, technology, and social trends reshape the way people live. The replacement of an icebox by an electric refrigerator represents just one of many changes. As often happens, change comes with gains and losses.

The change Hansi faces in the story may seem small now, but for him, that change signals a shift in daily life and the coming loss of a childhood pleasure. Over the next 25 years, icemen with horse-drawn wagons gradually disappeared from America's streets.

Yet many adults still fondly recall times when they followed the iceman and gathered chips from his wagon.

Licking blocks of ice on a hot day, c. 1910-1915.
Library of Congress Prints & Photographs Division,
George Grantham Bain Collection, LC-B2-2301-4.

Kennebec Ice wagon with school children, Birney Public School, Washington, DC, c. 1899
Library of Congress, Prints and Photographs Division,
Frances Benjamin Johnston Collection, LC-USZ62-4553